That's My Dad— He's a Hero!

GUY A. BORDEN

PAGE PUBLISHING, INC.
Conneaut Lake, PA

First originally published by Page Publishing 2021

ISBN 978-1-6624-5897-2 (pbk)
ISBN 978-1-6624-5898-9 (digital)

Printed in the United States of America

To the men who are called Dad.
Keep doing what you do because you do it so well!

Early one sunny Saturday morning, Britney and Jamal are sitting with their friends on the steps of their inner-city apartment with sad faces. They have nothing to do. Their father works all week driving a run-down, incredibly old minibus.

On this sunny Saturday morning, Britney and Jamal's father wants to play basketball with his buddies standing outside. He walks out of the apartment and sees his son and daughter with their friends sitting on the steps, saying sadly, "We do not have anything to do today!"

One of the children hollers, "Dad, what can you do to make this a good day?"

He hears them, and he feels sad. He thinks, *What can I do for them to smile and be happy?* Dad tells his buddies he is not going with them, saying, "I am taking the kids to the park with trees, picnic areas, and playgrounds."

Later, Mom loads up Dad's minibus with sandwiches, fruits, juices, water to drink, and the group of children. Dad says, "Everybody jump in!"

One of Britney and Jamal's friends is in a wheelchair, and he is on the minibus. Moms is with them too.

Now they are on the way to the park to have fun!

However, bad things start to happen. One, the minibus will not start. And so the children become sad again.

Another one of the children hollers, "Dad, what can you do to make this a good day?"

Dad says, "I will be back." He calls his basketball friends to help him get gas and a battery to start the minibus. And finally, it starts.

Britney and Jamal shout, "Hooray, we are on our way!"

Now they are really on the way, laughing and singing, "We are on our way!" as they go.

Suddenly, the sky starts to get dark. Now it is raining, lightning cracking across the sky, and the wind is blowing hard. They look out the minibus windows and stop laughing and singing.

Dad says, "Don't worry, the rain will stop." As he says the rain will stop, the lightning and winds stop too!

Byron says "Wow, he made the rain, lightning, and winds stop! He is a hero!"

Afterward, they start singing again and drive off. A few miles down the road, they hear a loud pop and the minibus stops rolling. "What is happening now?" Britney asks.

Dad gets out and sees a flat tire. The children are sad again. "Dad, what are you going to do now?"

Dad calls his basketball buddies again and asks them to bring a tire. They come fast and replace the tire. Britney and Jamal holler, "Dad is a hero! He can do anything!"

Now Dad drives the minibus into the park, down a winding road with trees' branches hanging into the road. The swinging branches look like they are attacking the minibus!

Rara hollers, "We are going to run into the tree branches!"

But like magic, the tree branches move out of the way. Dad drives down the road with no problem. Jamal shouts, "That's my dad—he's a hero!"

In the park, they meet Roger Ranger, who shows them a wonderful picnic area with the smell of pine.

The children get out of the minibus and begin to race down the curving trail to the picnic area.

Byron, in his wheelchair, speeds down the trail and wins the race. He shouts, "I win!"

Kim, running fast, falls and gets a bruised knee. Dad goes to the minibus and gets the first aid kit, then bandages the bruised knee. Britney and Jamal shout, "That's my dad—he's a hero!"

Then, everyone starts to burp. "We are hungry and thirsty!" they complain.

Dad and Mom pull out a grill, hot dogs, hamburgers, buns, chips, and drinks. The outdoor barbecue smells good. Fara says, "I cannot eat hot dogs and hamburgers because of my culture."

Dad tells her, "We have banana fritters just for you."

Britney and Jamal shout, "That's my dad—he's a hero!"

Much later, they are leaving the park, and all are singing in the minibus, "That's my dad—he's a hero!"

Finally, they arrive home at the steps of their inner-city apartment with happy faces. They've had lots of fun outdoors in the park.

Later, Dad muses, *What can I do for them to smile and be happy? Hmm. I know! I will be a hero!*

About the Author

Guy A. Borden graduated from the University of the District of Columbia with a bachelor of business administration in 1998. He received an associate degree in applied science in early childhood development from Baltimore City Community College in 2018, when he was seventy-one years of age. He has since retired from working in the federal government, often volunteers, and can receive senior citizen's discounts.

CPSIA information can be obtained
at www.ICGtesting.com
Printed in the USA
LVHW070924040422
715245LV00006B/74